I0820502

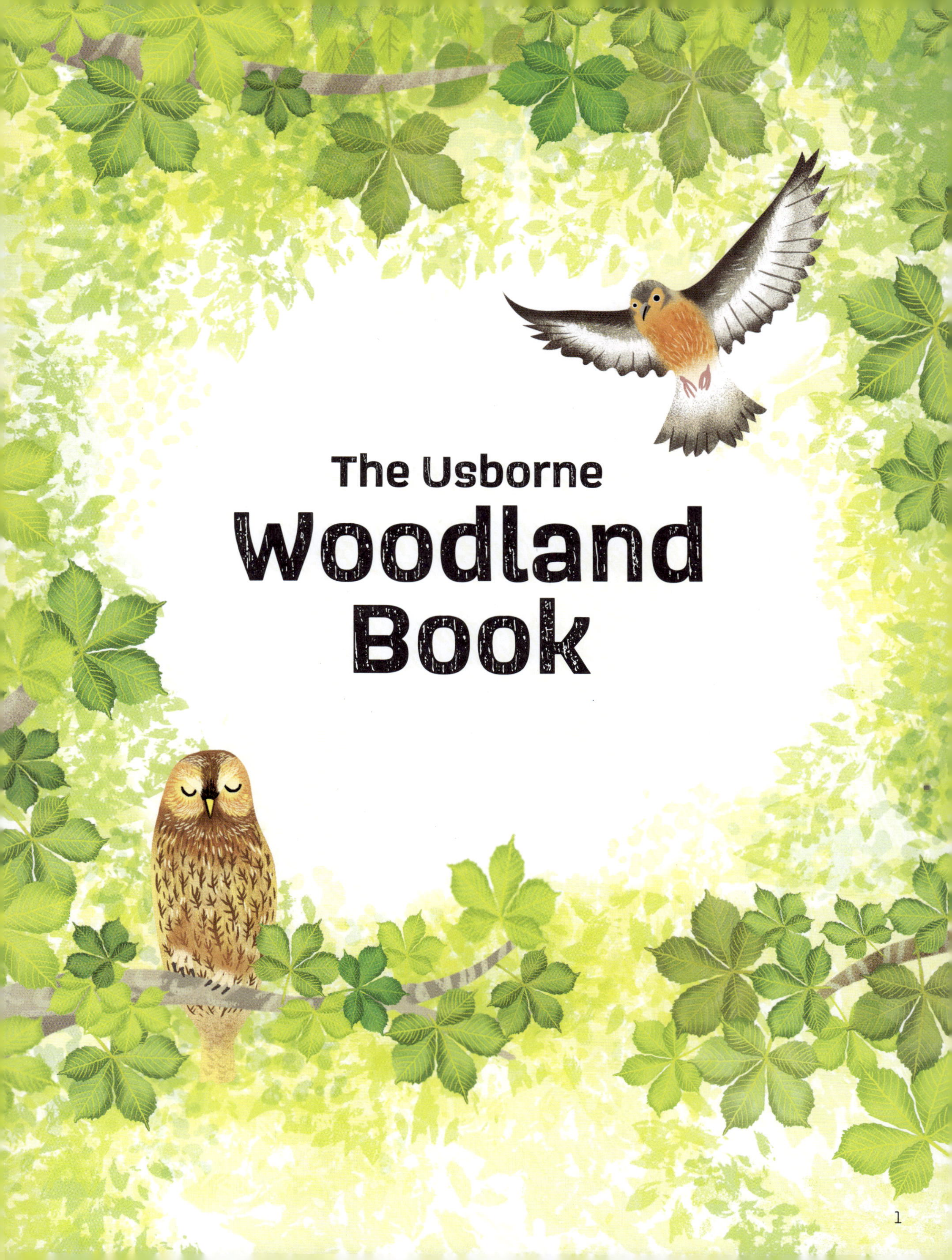

The Usborne Woodland Book

Usborne Quicklinks

For links to websites where you can explore woodlands around the world and through the seasons and discover all sorts of creatures that live in them, go to **usborne.com/Quicklinks** and type in the keywords "woodland book".

Usborne Publishing is not responsible for the content of external websites. Children should be supervised online. Please follow the online safety guidelines at Usborne Quicklinks.

The Usborne Woodland Book

Illustrated by Nat Hues

Written by Emily Bone and Alice James

Designed by Helen Edmonds,
Anna Gould and Zoe Wray

Woodland consultant: Laura McConnell
Wildlife expert: Zoë Simmons

Guide to the woodland book

You are here

Be introduced to a **woodland** on pages 6-7.

Explore a **summer woodland** on pages 8-9.

Use your senses to **feel, smell and listen** to the woods on pages 10-11.

On pages 12-13, discover **all sorts of leaves.**

Be a woodland bird watcher on pages 14-15.

Find out which **creatures** live in the woods on pages 16-21.

See what happens to the woods **as summer ends** on pages 22-25.

Find out about **woodland shelters** on pages 26-27.

Discover mysterious **mushrooms** on pages 28-29.

Learn about woodland creepy crawlies that live **up high** and **down low** on pages 30-33.

What are **ancient woods?** Find out on pages 34-35.

Make a **memory twig** and **picture map** on pages 36-37.
Spend a day in the woods making a **woodland journal** on pages 38-39.
In the woods when darkness falls, tell stories among the **silhouettes and shadows** on pages 40-41.
Then, explore the woods **at night** on pages 42-43.
Learn how **explorers navigate** on pages 48-49.
Brrr! Visit a **winter woodland** on pages 44-47.
It's **Springtime** on pages 50-51.
Tell **woodland tales and legends** on pages 52-53.
After you read pages 54-57, you'll be a **tree** expert.
There's a useful **Woodland glossary** on pages 58-61 and you'll find the **index** on pages 62-63.

All kinds of creatures make the woods their home - from squirrels and birds in the treetops to scuttling creepy crawlies in the undergrowth.

A woodland can be anything from a vast forest full of thousands of trees, to a little wooded area in your local park. Most woods are a mix of different types of trees, along with a tangle of other plants - shrubs, vines, ferns, flowers and mosses.

Many tales, myths and stories have been set in woods. Woods can feel dark and mysterious, or exciting and full of adventures. Step between the trees, look up at the tall branches, feel the cool, shady air and go exploring.

Ferns often carpet the ground, along with woodland wildflowers in the spring.

Some woodlands have trees that are hundreds, maybe even thousands, of years old.

This little symbol highlights an important safety or environmental warning.

If you do visit the woods, make sure you stay safe. Carry water, a map and a fully charged phone and never go anywhere without a responsible grown-up. Don't pick any plants or flowers, and try to leave everything as you found it, too.

In a summer woodland,

a canopy of leafy branches stretches out to create shade on the damp ground. Old trees soar high above scrubby bushes, twisting vines, young saplings, and delicate woodland flowers.

Look up and down and notice the different things around you.

The strong, high branches of tall trees stretch up and out. The leaves angle themselves so they're bathed in sunlight.

Thick, gnarled bark protects the tree trunk and branches. One layer of wood grows inside the trunk each year, making the bark outside expand and crack.

The top of a tree is called its crown.

Look out for big birds, such as birds of prey, perching up here.

Leaves take in light, air and water to make food and help the tree grow.

Vines wind their way up, trying to get to the sunlight.

Dogwood
Virginia creeper
A sturdy trunk supports the branches and takes water up to the leaves.
Young trees, called saplings
Bushes and small trees grow well in the shade.
The shady woodland floor feels spongy underfoot because it's made up of layers of soft leaves, wood and dead plants. These rot down and create food for trees and other plants.
Frilly green plants, called ferns
Mosses are plants that grow in thick clumps on damp ground.
Woodland flowers grow in patches of sunlight.
Virginia waterleaf
Huge roots run deep into the ground. They keep the tree upright and suck up water and nutrients from the soil.

Feel, smell and listen

to the woods. Close your eyes to let your other senses do the exploring.

Feel the bark on different tree trunks. What is the texture like?

Smell the woods around you by standing still and taking some deep breaths.

Can you tell what the weather's been like? Does it smell like wet plants or dry, dusty ground?

Listen: what can you hear? Some animals, such as deer, have big ears so they can hear things from far away. Cup your hands around your ears to make your own deer ears.

All sorts of leaves grow in woodlands.

The leaves of some trees, called deciduous trees, turn yellow or red in autumn, and drop to the floor. Other trees, called evergreens, keep leaves on their branches all year. Here are some common leaf shapes, and the types of trees you'll find them on.

Hand-shaped leaves
• Horse chestnut
• Sycamore
• Maple
Horse chestnut leaves five sections known as 'fingers'.
Maple leaves turn a vivid red before they fall.
Lots of leaves on one stem
• Elder
• Ash
Ash leaves fall when they are still green - they don't turn red or orange beforehand.
Little leaves on one stem like this are known as leaflets.
Soft fan-like fronds
• Cedar
• Sequoia
• Cypress
For help identifying leaves go to the Usborne **Quicklinks** website (see front of book).

Be a woodland bird watcher

and learn how to spot birds hidden in leafy, shady trees. Sit quietly and *look up* for these different birds. You could close your eyes and *listen*, too.

Notice little birds flitting from branch to branch, or hanging upside down picking off bugs, seeds and berries. These are probably finches and tits.

Some birds will chatter in groups, while others will stand on their own and give a long, trilling call.

You'd never see all these birds in one place. To identify which bird you've spotted, you need to look closely at its markings and size, and listen to its call, too.

Caw, caw
Crow
Peer up above the treetops. You might spot crows or birds of prey, such as buzzards and sparrowhawks, soaring in the sky.
Owls are awake at night, but in the day some will sit on shady branches, close to tree trunks.
In spring, try to find a bird flying to and from one spot. It might have a nest full of hungry chicks there.
Jay's nest
Cheep, cheep
Nuthatch
Woodpeckers, treecreepers and nuthatches hop up, down and around tree trunks, looking for bugs to eat.
All kinds of birds root around in leaves seeking out tasty grubs, nuts and seeds on the woodland floor.
Pigeon
Jay
Woodpeckers

Woodland creatures are more likely to hide in or behind trees than be out in the open.
Woodmouse
Hare
Deer
Sit or stand very still so you can search silently for creatures. If you don't move or make much noise some animals might make an appearance.
Boar
ZZZZZ
Bears sleep in hollows under big trees.
Snake
Snakes and lizards need heat from the sun to move. So look for them basking in open clearings.
Lizard
Worm
Caterpillar
Lots of creepy crawlies live in the undergrowth.
Spider
Beetle

Birds and squirrels build nests out of sticks and moss among the branches.
Look up among the branches for birds, insects and squirrels. They might be flying or scampering around, or resting on twigs and leaves.
Owls and bats sleep in trees. Look out for holes and hollows where they might be resting.
Beaver lodge
Some animals make their homes in or near woodland rivers.
Badger sett
Rabbit
Stoat
Pine marten
Rabbit warren
Vole
Explore the floor for holes dug into the mud. Lots of woodland creatures live in burrows underground.
Cicada
You won't see all these animals in the same place - they live in different woodlands around the world.
Chipmunk burrow

Footprints can give a clue to the creatures that might be nearby. Following the trails left by animals is called tracking. The clearest tracks are left in mud where the ground is soft, so search for footprints in a muddy woodland.

Which direction was the animal heading? How many sets of footprints can you see? Was there just one or a group? How can you tell?

If there's a river or stream running through the woods, look out for duck, otter or beaver prints.
Duck
Otter
Beaver
In some animals, such as rabbits, the prints of their front and back feet are distinctly different.
Front
Rabbit
Back
Fox
Bear

Woodland animals leave lots of clues, including droppings, hair, and marks on trees, as well as footprints.

Long dark hairs, caught on brambles or fences

Path dug under a bush or tree

Sloppy piles of dung, in holes in the ground

Badgers often leave all their dung together outside their setts.

Clues that a **badger** has been nearby...

Claw scratch marks on fallen logs

Tufts of pale fur caught on a fence

Low twigs that have been munched

Warrens dug in the ground near the base of trees

Signs left by a **rabbit**...

Small grassy pellets of dung

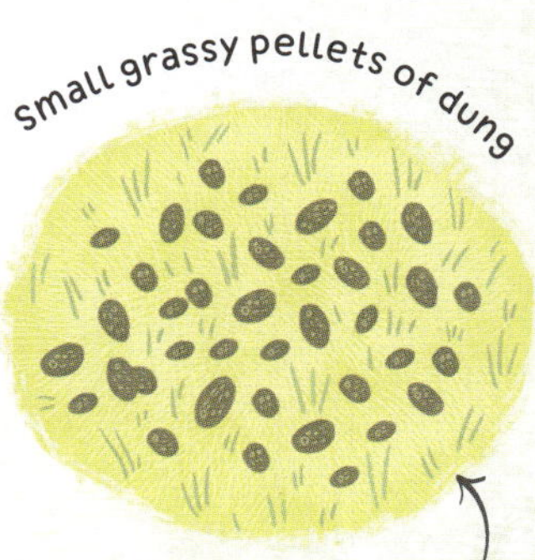

Scientists call dung they use for identification scat.

As summer ends, the weather gets cooler and the woods begin to change again. Ripe fruits, nuts and seeds drop to the ground for hungry woodland animals to eat. Leaves start to turn red, orange and yellow, and gradually flutter off the trees.

Go on a fall walk to look for signs of the new season. See if you can spot some of the things below...

A tree's seeds come in all sorts of shapes and sizes, and some have protective cases. A seed contains the ingredients for a brand new tree. Seeds drop to the ground late in the year, and some eventually grow into new trees.

Nuts are tough cases that protect a precious seed inside.

Oak nuts are called acorns.

Squirrels bury acorns to eat in the winter. They often forget them, and the acorns are left to grow into new oaks.

Pine trees grow cones full of seeds late in summer.

Hazelnuts drop to the floor, and some get eaten by birds.

When the cones open up, seeds are blown away by the wind, and scatter widely on the ground.

Some trees grow **fruits** around their seeds, to attract animals to eat them. After animals digest the fruit, the seeds end up on the woodland floor and start to grow.
Crab apple
Crab apple
Blackthorn
Sloe
Blackthorn fruits are called sloes. The seed in a sloe is inside a hard case called a pit.
Berries are small fruits with tiny seeds inside.
Maple
Maple seeds, called keys, spiral down to the ground in the wind.
Key
Mountain Ash
Clusters of bright red berries

Woodland shelters

used to be built by forest dwellers to sleep in, rest in or keep dry in a storm.

Tree teepees have branches propped in a circle, around a tree trunk.

Teepees can provide cool shade when it's hot outside, and some shelter from the wind when it's cold.

The sticks need to be tall enough for a person to fit inside.

The ground inside is cleared to make it more comfy.

Stick shelters are built around a main branch wedged between two trees.
Sticks are propped against the main branch, along both sides.
Leaf huts can be warm and waterproof.
Sides are packed with leaves, ferns and twigs.
Leaf huts are a triangular shape. They're widest at the entrance and narrowest at the back. So a person can fit in lying down, with their head at the front.
A backpack can be used to close up the entrance and keep out the cold.

Mushrooms pop up in woods in spring and late summer. They are the fruits of underground living things called fungi. All kinds of wonderfully named varieties grow on the shady woodland floor, on soggy rotten wood and damp tree trunks.

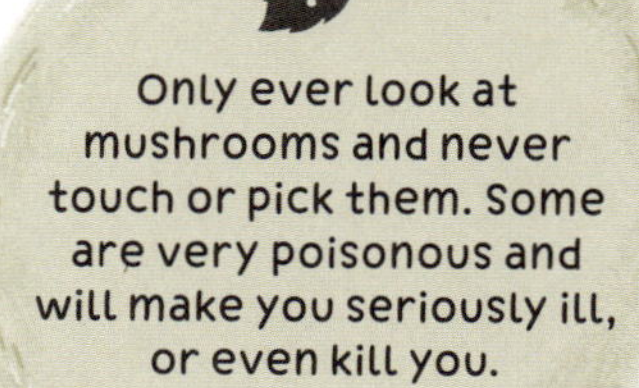

Only ever look at mushrooms and never touch or pick them. Some are very poisonous and will make you seriously ill, or even kill you.

Jelly ear really do look like little ears. Look for them growing on trees in spring.

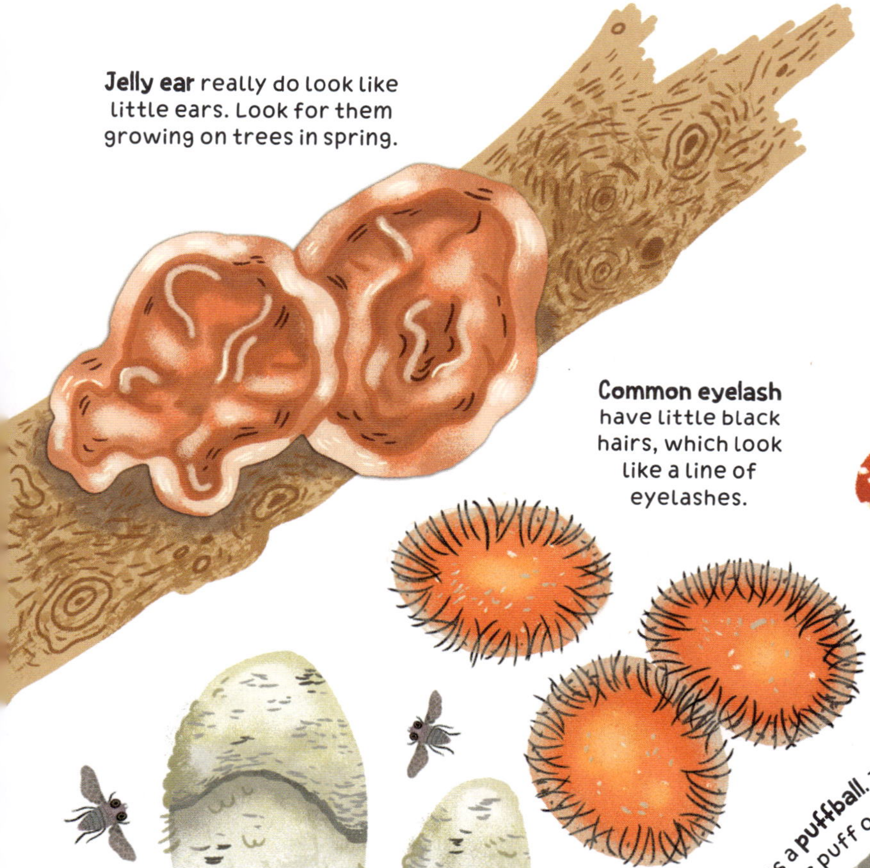

Fly agaric mushrooms are shiny and bright red with white speckles.

Common eyelash have little black hairs, which look like a line of eyelashes.

This big round mushroom is a **puffball**. These mushrooms explode, and their seeds puff out in a big cloud.

Long, white stalks

Stinkhorn smell horribly rotten. Mushroom seeds, called spores, are tiny. The smell attracts flies, which then help to spread the spores on their feet.

Candlesnuff or **stag's horn fungus** has lots of spiky prongs.

Amethyst deceivers start off bright purple and turn pale as they grow bigger.

Honey fungus feeds on tree roots.

Look for mushrooms growing in big circles, known as **fairy rings**.

People used to think these were made by dancing fairies. Stepping inside brings bad luck, unless you run around the ring 9 times first.

Shaggy parasol

Dead man's fingers look like hands poking out of the ground.

Witches' butter grows as bright yellow squiggly patches on trees.

Up high in the woods in late spring or summer, there will be hundreds of different bugs flying, hopping and crawling in the trees.

If you shake a branch you can take a closer look at bugs living there. You could put a few white sheets of paper under a tree or low-hanging branch. Gently shake the tree, wait for 5-10 seconds, and a few bugs should fall on the paper. Remember, never touch the bugs, and leave them alone to go back to their homes.

Down low on the leafy woodland floor, bugs and other creatures scuttle, slither, hop or burrow in and under crumbly rotting wood. Find a stick and carefully lift up a fallen branch or log to look underneath. Remember to put the log back in its place again.

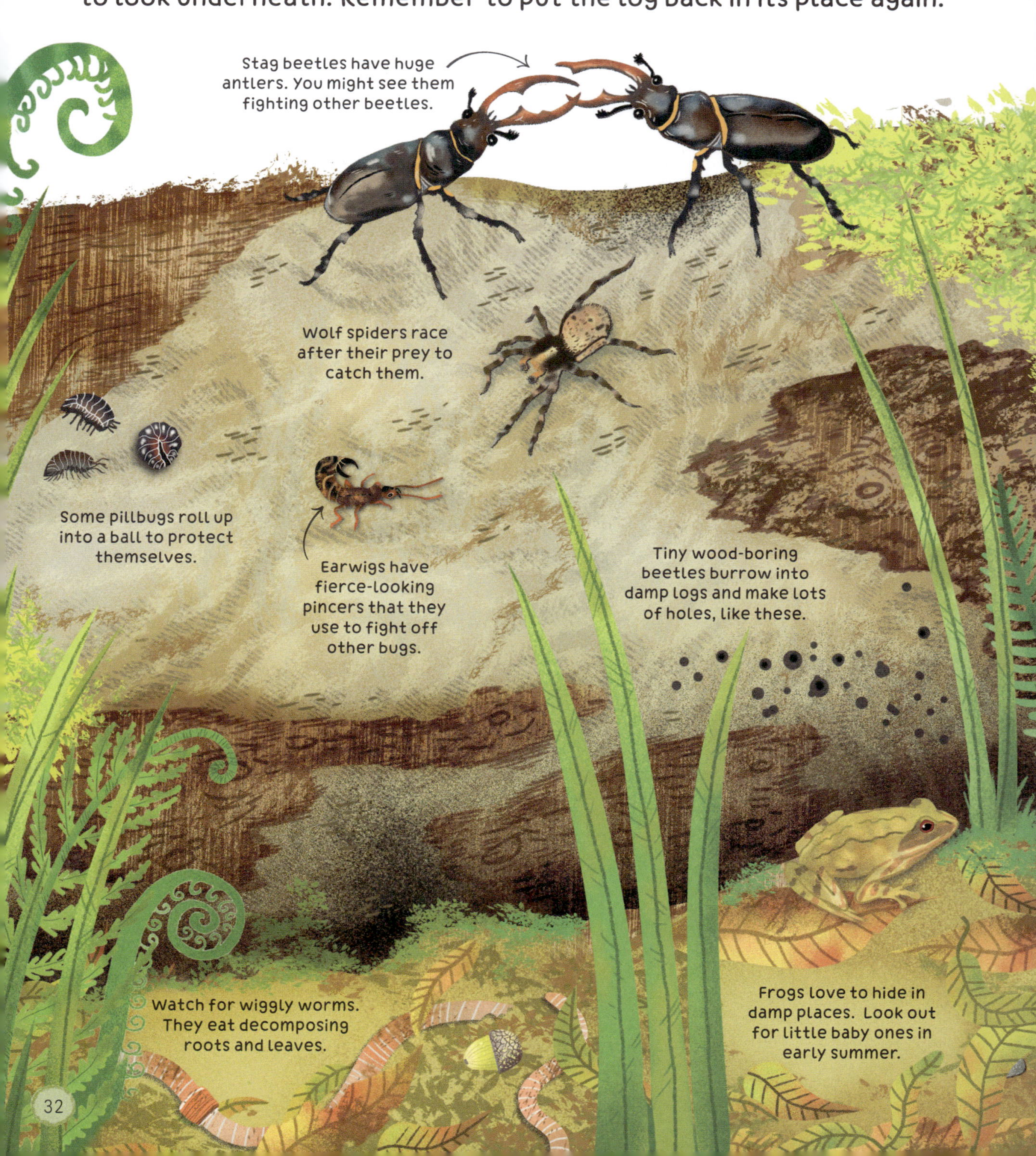

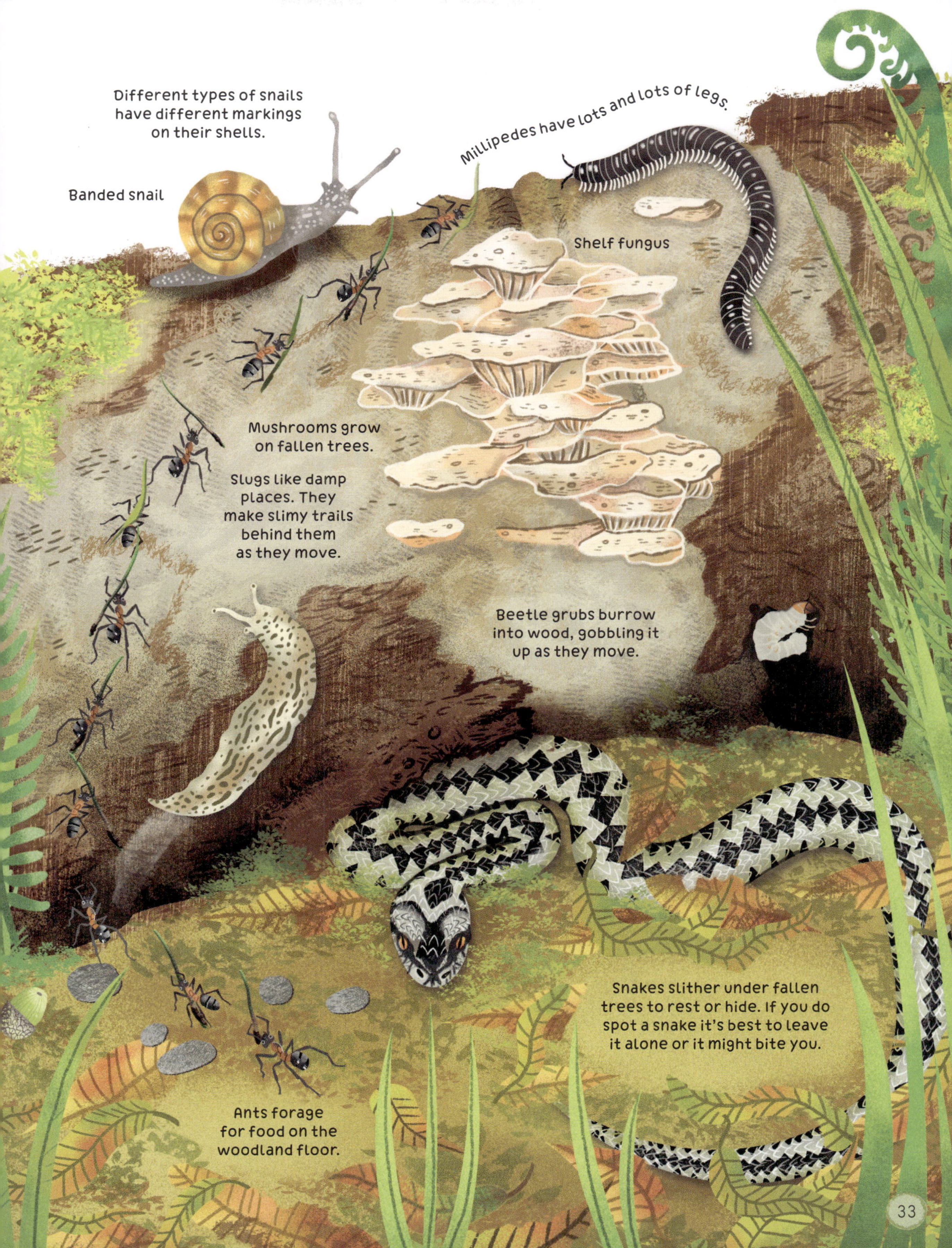
Different types of snails have different markings on their shells.
Banded snail
Millipedes have lots and lots of legs.
Shelf fungus
Mushrooms grow on fallen trees.
Slugs like damp places. They make slimy trails behind them as they move.
Beetle grubs burrow into wood, gobbling it up as they move.
Snakes slither under fallen trees to rest or hide. If you do spot a snake it's best to leave it alone or it might bite you.
Ants forage for food on the woodland floor.

Some woods are ancient - they've been growing in the same place for hundreds of years. Look out for interesting, characterful trees and signs that people have lived in the woods.

Ancient woods are usually a higgledy-piggledy mix of different trees, with lots of other plants growing around them.

Woodland wildflowers prefer ground that hasn't been disturbed for a long time, so they're more likely to grow in ancient woods.

Look for signs of past forest-dwellers, such as a clearing, walls, mounds, pits or anything else that seems out of place.

Trees with lots of thin trunks are called coppices. Years ago, they were cut down to stumps, which made them grow like this. Then, they were cut down again to be used as fence posts.

Ancient trees

are gnarled, bumpy and often crooked. The bark has lots of splits, hollows and holes. Imagine what kind of a life the tree has had, and all the things it's seen.

Up in the branches

you might see jagged breaks where parts of an old tree have died and broken off.

Mushrooms, mosses and liverworts - unusual flat, green plants - like to live on and around old trees.

Hug a tree to get a rough idea of how old it is.

If you and a friend can put your arms around a trunk and not touch fingers, the tree might be over 100 years old.

An oak that has a trunk two hugs wide is roughly 150 years old.

Look out for animals nesting in holes and creepy crawlies darting in and out of the bark, eating old, rotting wood.

Explore the woods while you're on a walk, by collecting interesting things or making a picture map.

Make a memory twig.

Go on a short walk and collect things that will remind you about what you've seen and the route you've taken. Tie each one to a twig as you walk along, starting from the bottom and going up the twig.

Never go out walking in the woods unless you have a grown-up with you. It's safest to carry a map, too.

Never pick any living plant, and scatter any objects you've collected before you leave.

Make a picture map inspired by what you've seen on a woodland walk. Add different trees, landmarks, hilly areas and anything else you think is interesting.

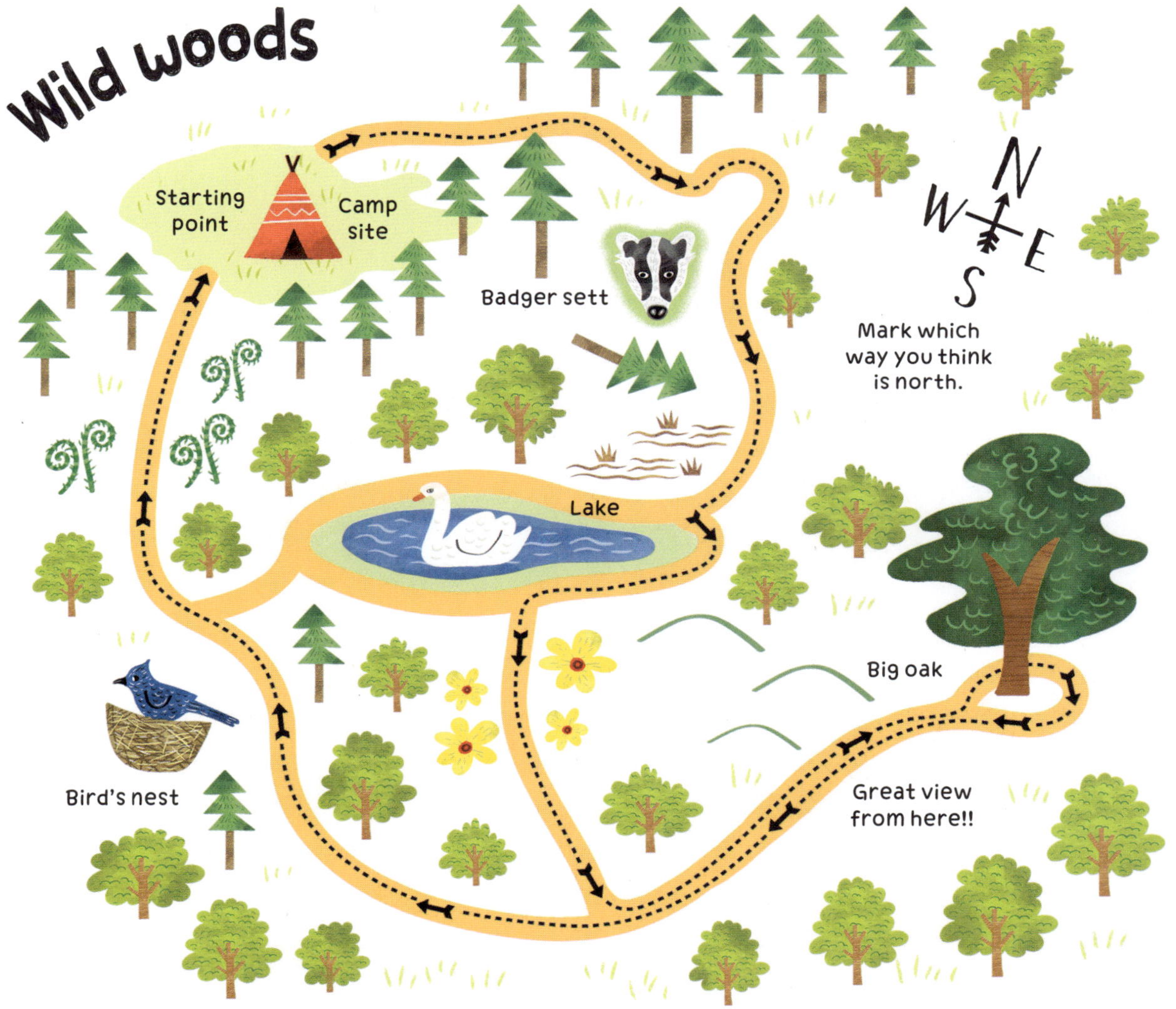

Wild woods

Starting point

Camp site

Badger sett

Mark which way you think is north.

N
W
E
S

Lake

Big oak

Bird's nest

Great view from here!!

Include a key to explain the different things on your map:

Pine trees	Fallen tree	Route	Woodland flowers	Boggy ground	Beech trees	Hills	Ferns

Write a woodland journal.

If you're camping in the woods (or staying nearby), it's a chance to get up early and spend the whole day from sunrise to sunset being super-observant. Make a sketch or note of the things you see, hear and smell. You could write more next time you go to the woods.

BLUEBELL FOREST CAMPING TRIP

DAY 1:

MORNING

The sun rose at 6:30 this morning.

Birds singing very loudly.

ANIMALS I SPOTTED THIS MORNING

4 rabbits

1 deer (wow!)

Birds hopping around in tree branches.

Spider weaving a web - very pretty!

What time does the sun rise?

Very early after the sun rises, listen to the birds singing.

Can you hear the same call over and over again?
Or a mixture of different ones?
Which birds do you see first?
What are they doing?

Early in the morning, look out for rabbits and deer, nibbling on grass and plants. Do you see any other animals?

Early morning water droplets on grass, or glistening on trees and spider webs, is called dew. It's made by the cool night air meeting the warming morning sun.

Take a note of what you see on a walk.

If you can see the sky through the trees, do you notice any clouds? What are they like?

What times of day do you see most birds and insects?

How many plants and trees can you identify?

These dark clouds could mean rain is on the way.

Do plants or trees change throughout the day? Do some droop in the heat, or sway more in the wind?

AFTERNOON:

At 3pm black clouds through the trees followed by a shower of rain. Couldn't see many insects or birds. After the rain stopped, saw lots of bees and flies.

EVENING:

Sunset at 8:30pm. Twit-twoo noises - owls? Back at the campsite we watched bats swooping overhead, told stories and sang songs.

Sheltered under an oak tree.

When does the sun set each day,

and when does it start to get dark?

As the sun sets, birds are getting ready to sleep. You might see crows circling and calling.

Can you see any night animals waking up, such as bats and owls?

Silhouettes and shadows

appear as dusk draws in, and the setting sun streams through the trees.

You could tell stories as the sun sets. All kinds of tales, from ghost stories to fairy tales, use the woods as a setting. Tell a story using one of these starters:

It was a still, warm night. They could hear different creatures rustling, snuffling and hooting among the dark trees...

She dashed through the forest, dodging trees and ducking under branches...

He knelt to the floor and looked at the footprints. "What type of animal came through here?" he wondered aloud...

See page 52-53 for more woodland story-telling.

The evening sky can give you clues about tomorrow's weather.
"A ring around the moon, rain's coming soon"
"Red sky at night, shepherd's delight"
Sayings like this are known as weatherlore. A red or pink evening sky means tomorrow's weather will be dry. Shepherds and sailors watch the sky closely, to know how they'll be affected by the weather.
Look for frosty, pale rings around the evening moon - it means there's moisture in the air, and rain could be on its way.
You could send light messages in the dark, by turning a lamp on and off.
Try coming up with a few signals to send to your friends or family.
Long flash = Meet you outside!
2 short flashes = Shh, I can hear an animal.

At night the woods come alive with a new set of creatures - ones that sleep during the day and are awake at night, known as nocturnal creatures. This is the twilight world of bats, moths, and twinkling fireflies.

If you trek through the woods as it gets dark, you might hear and see these nocturnal animals. (But never go out at night without a grown-up.)

Through the canopy, stars twinkle high in the sky. Stars are most visible on clear nights, in places without any streetlights.

Lots of creatures are attracted to light. If you leave a light on the ground for a few minutes, insects will often gather around it.

A winter woodland on a cold, frosty day, can look bare and empty. But, even in the depths of winter, the woods are alive with different plants, and animals seeking food. Here are some things to look out for...

Animals will venture further in search of food in winter so you're more likely to see them.
If there's snow or frost, look out for animal footprints.
Holly has spiky leaves and bright red berries.
waxwings
Flocks of birds feed on berries that grew in late summer.
Mountain ash berries
When it's really cold, spiky icicles may form as water droplets freeze on tree branches.
Ivy grows berries which birds love to eat.
Witches' brooms are masses of shoots growing out from tree branches. This happens when the tree is damaged or has a disease.

When a tree's leaves have fallen in winter, look at the shade and texture of the **bark** around its wooden trunk.

Here are some of the most common types of bark and where to find them.

Bumpy and dotted with holes

- Poplar
- Hazel

Poplar bark

Spotted bark that looks like scales

- Oak
- Maple
- Spruce
- Hawthorn

This is the bark of an oak tree. It gets more knobbly, gnarled and knotted over time.

Smooth or gently bumpy

- Beech
- Mountain ash
- Holly

Beech bark

Beech trees often have pieces of bark missing - squirrels use strips of the smooth bark in their nests.

Rough and red
• Juniper
• Sequoia
Juniper bark
Vertical lines or diamonds
• Horse chestnut
• Hornbeam
• Ash
• Willow
Horse chestnut bark
Birch trees shed layers of their papery bark. Can you find any pieces peeling off?
Pale and papery
• Birch
• Aspen
Patchy
• Plane
• Sycamore
• Yew
The patchy pattern on plane tree bark inspired some designs of camouflage clothing in the Second World War.
Get a closer look at a bark's texture by making a bark rubbing. Hold a piece of paper against a trunk, and rub over it with a pencil or crayon.

Explorers navigate

through woods using all sorts of techniques. Finding their way and not getting lost often relies on being able to work out which direction they're facing - north, south, east or west.

The **stars** have helped people navigate for centuries.

In the Northern Hemisphere, the North Star shines over the North Pole.

In the Southern Hemisphere, the Southern Cross (Crux) points south.

Explorers also make note of any landmarks, or features of the landscape, such as a river. They can match these to a map, or follow them to find their way back.

Sun and shade influence the way things grow, which gives clues too. In the Northern Hemisphere, it's sunnier on the south side, and shadier on the north side.

The side of a tree that gets most sun usually grows best. Look out for asymmetric trees - the biggest side probably points south.

The sun rises in the east, and sets in the west, everywhere in the world.

Leaves on the shady north side tend to be larger and darker than on the south side. They are bigger to get enough sunlight to make energy.

Moss grows best in moist places. It's usually damper and darker on the north side of trees, where there's less sun.

In the Southern Hemisphere, these will be flipped - the north side is brighter and the south side is darker.

Find your way using just a stick and a couple of stones.

Push a long stick upright into the ground on a sunny day, and put a stone at the end of its shadow. Wait 15 minutes, then put another stone at the end of its shadow, which will have moved. Draw an imaginary line between the two stones. Following that line, the first stone points west and the second stone points east.

Springtime! At the end of winter, warm sunlight streams into the woods. Bare branches burst into life again. New buds, woodland flowers and shoots appear, along with busy birds, and the first bees and butterflies.

Fluffy, dangling flowers, called catkins, grow on some trees, including hazel and willow.
The word catkin comes from the Dutch for kitten, 'katteken', because they look like kittens' tails.
Hazel catkins
Birds hop and fly around collecting twigs, moss and other things to make their nests.
Budbursts are buds that have just opened into brand new leaves.
Wild garlic has spiky white flowers.
Elder budburst
Ferns are frondy woodland plants that die in winter and grow again in spring.
Trilliums have three leaves and bright white flowers with three petals.
Their spiral-shaped leaves slowly uncurl as they grow.
You'll probably smell the oniony scent of wild garlic before you see it!

Tales and legends are often set in woods, because they can seem like mysterious places where people get lost, things lurk in the darkness, and magic happens...

Lots of **fairy tales** take place in woods.

Rapunzel was locked away in a tall tower, deep in the heart of the woods...

You could try writing your own story set in the woods. Are the woods threatening and dark, or peaceful and full of kind, woodland creatures?

Little Red Riding Hood walked through the woods to visit her grandmother...

Hansel and Gretel scattered breadcrumbs through the woods...

Light-carrying creatures appear in woodland stories from all over the world.

The characters carry misty lights that lead people off safe paths. These cunning creatures have all sorts of names.

Scientists think these eerie lights might actually be from real creatures that light up - fireflies, glow-worms, or the flash of an owl's white feathers.

For hundreds of years, all around the world, people have told **myths and folk tales** full of magic, mighty trees.

In Viking mythology, a great ash tree called Yggdrasil reached to the sky, and linked the Viking world together.

Look around at trunks to see if you can find bumps, knobs and knots that look like faces. How do they look? Sleepy, wise, angry?

Druids, religious leaders of ancient European people called the Celts, named themselves after 'druir' - an oak tree.

Oak trees live so long that in many myths and folk tales they are considered powerful and wise. They live about 50 years before they even start producing acorns.

Zeus, king of the Ancient Greek gods, and Jupiter, king of the Ancient Roman gods, were thought to control the sky and storms. They were both associated with oak trees, too. Scientists have discovered that oak trees are more likely to be struck by lightning than any other tree.

Trees, trees, as far as the eye can see...

Woodlands are full of different trees, from huge spreading oaks to thin wispy birches and tall spiky pines. Here are some of the trees mentioned in this book.

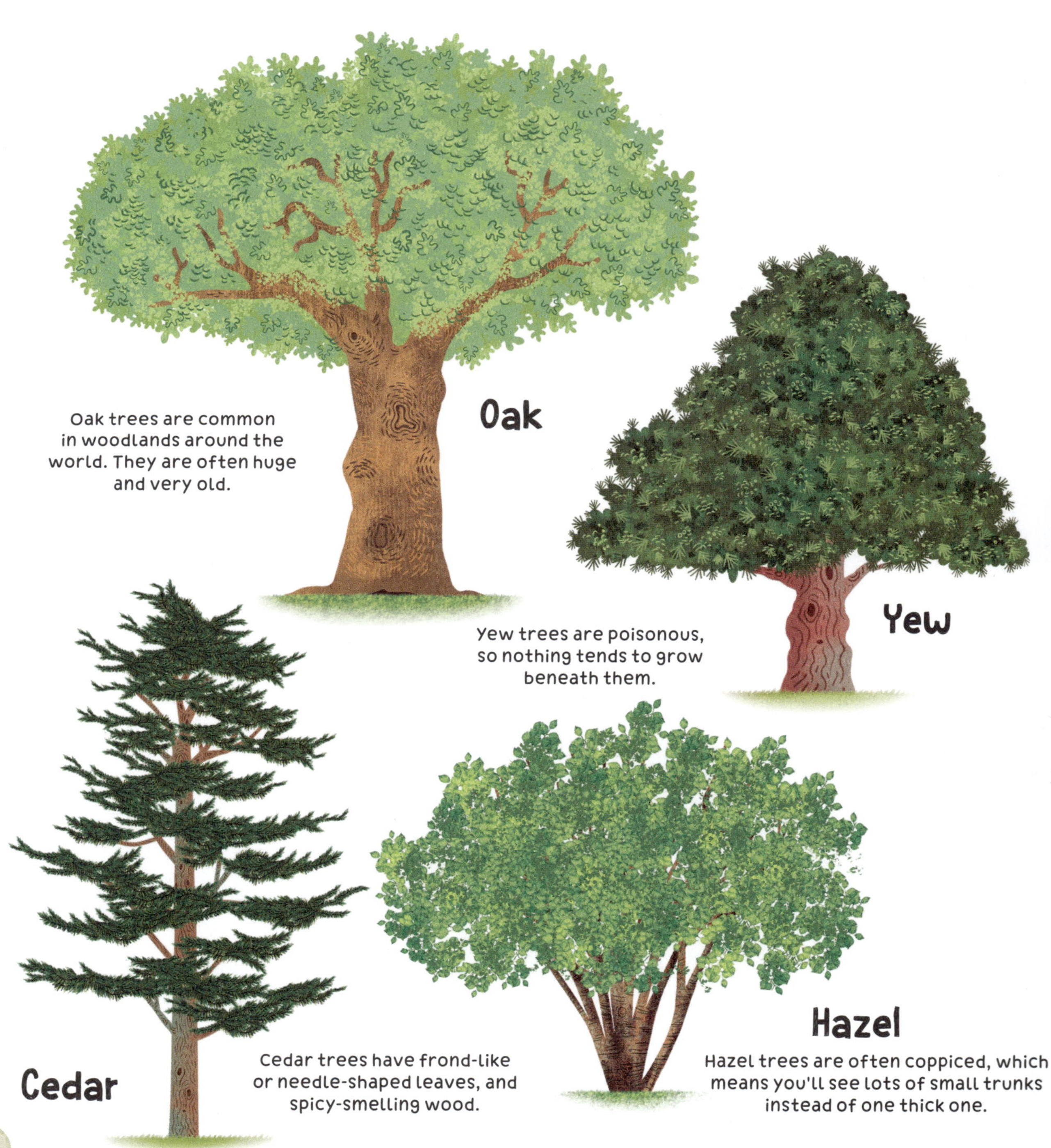

Cherry trees bloom spectacularly, with clouds of pink and white blossom erupting all together. Leaves start to grow at the same time.
Blackthorn
The branches of blackthorn and cherry trees are laden with flowers in the spring, and fruits later in the year.
Horse chestnut
Cherry
Fir
Pine
Fir, pine and spruce are all types of evergreen trees known as conifers. They have spiky needle-shaped leaves and wooden cones full of seeds.
Horse chestnut trees are easiest to identify by their leaves and seeds. They have leaves like five long fingers (see page 13) and prickly seed cases.

European sycamore and maple trees are very common in woodlands.

The leaves of most deciduous woodland trees turn yellow or orange late in the year, and then drop to the ground.

Aspen and birch trees look very similar from a distance. They're both tall, with pale bark and green leaves that go yellow in the fall. Tell them apart by their leaves (see page 12).

Juniper
Some types of juniper grow into tall, twisted trees like this one, while others form bushes, covered in berries. Junipers have needle leaves, and strong-smelling bark.
Sequoia
Sequoia trees, also known as giant redwoods, form huge, towering forests in America. They are the largest trees in the world.
Elder
Elder trees grow clusters of white flowers that birds and butterflies like to feed on.
Scot's pine
Holly

Glossary

Here are some useful woodland words.

ancient woodland - woods that have been growing in the same place for hundreds of years.

bark - a tough layer covering a tree's trunk and branches to protect them. Bark looks different depending on the type of tree, so it's also used to help with identification.

blossom - flowers that grow on fruit trees, such as crab apple and cherry, in the spring.

bud - a little growth on a woodland plant that opens up into a leaf or flower.

canopy - the highest branches, which stretch out. In summer, canopies often block out the sunlight.

catkins - dangling flowers that grow on some trees, such as hazel and birch.

clearing - an open space in a woodland that was probably made when trees were cut down years ago to make space for grazing cattle or building homes.

compass - a tool with a little needle that points north. It's used for finding your way in the woods.

coppice - a tree, usually hazel or ash, that has been grown to have lots of thin trunks rather than one thick one. The trunks are cut down to make fences.

crown - the very top of a tree.

deciduous - a tree or plant that loses its leaves in the winter.

evergreen - a tree or plant that keeps its leaves through the winter. Leaves are usually thick and glossy, or pointy needles.

ferns - green plants with feathery, frondy leaves that grow on the woodland floor.

folklore - beliefs or stories relating to a particular place or thing, which have been passed down through generations.

frond - the feathery leaves of ferns and some evergreen trees, usually made up of lots of small leaves.

fruit - the fleshy surroundings some trees grow to contain their seeds. Animals eat fruit and spread the seeds in their droppings.

grub - a young insect, usually a beetle.

leaf skeleton - when all the softer parts of a fallen leaf break down in the winter and only the stem and veins are left behind.

lichen - a flat, crusty-feeling, greenish-yellow plant that grows on shady tree trunks and walls.

liverwort - a green plant that grows on trees. A liverwort has lots of small, flat green leaves.

moss - a small green plant that grows in damp places. It usually covers tree trunks and roots, damp ground and rocks in a woodland.

mushroom - the fruits of underground living things. Mushrooms grow above ground in spring or from late summer. There are lots of different varieties.

nectar - a sweet liquid inside flowers. Bees, butterflies and other insects feed on nectar.

nocturnal - animals that are awake at night and sleep during the day.

nut - a seed with a hard case that grows from flowers on some trees. If nuts are buried in the ground, they will grow into new trees.

pine cone - the fruit of a pine tree. Seeds called pine nuts grow inside them.

pollen - a dusty yellow powder inside flowers. When pollen is spread from one flower to another, it makes the plant or tree grow new seeds, nuts or fruits.

roots - the part of a tree that stretches down into the ground to hold it upright and suck up water and food from the soil.

sapling - a young tree.

scat - animal droppings.

seed - what a plant produces to grow new plants. Seeds grow from flowers, and are sometimes inside fruits or hard cases, called nuts.

sett - a badger's underground home.

tracking - looking for signs of where an animal has been in a wood.

trunk - thick, sturdy part of a tree which holds up the branches and takes water up to them.

veins - little tubes that run through each leaf of a plant or tree carrying water and food.

warren - the underground home of rabbits.

wildflowers - spring or summer flowers that grow on the woodland floor, usually in areas where sunlight streams in through the trees.

witches' brooms - lots of twigs sprouting out of branches on a tree. This usually happens because the tree has a disease.

Index

Managing Designer: Zoe Wray

Edited by Jane Chisholm

Digital manipulation by John Russell

This edition first published in 2025. AE. First published in America 2018.